STREET FOOTBALL

DARICE BAILER

The Child's World®
childsworld.com

Published by The Child's World®
1980 Lookout Drive • Mankato, MN 56003-1705
800-599-READ • www.childsworld.com

Photo Credits
© abhbah05/Adobe Stock: 17; Andrey Popov/
Adobe Stock: 4-5; Fotokostic/Shutterstock.com:
6; Jeramey Lende/Alamy Stock Photo: 9; John
Terence Turner/Alamy Stock Photo: cover; OlegVer/
Shutterstock.com: 18; RTimages/Shutterstock.com:
13; SUDIO 1ONE/Adobe Stock: 10, 14; ZUMA
Press Inc./Alamy Stock Photo: 21

ISBN: 9781503823730
LCCN: 2017944872

Printed in the United States of America
PA2356

ABOUT THE AUTHOR

Darice Bailer has wanted to be a writer since she was in fifth grade. Today she is the author of many books for young readers. She lives in Kansas with her husband.

TABLE OF CONTENTS

GET MOVING!

Football is fun and good exercise. You can play in a park. A yard. Or behind your school.

FUN FACT

In street football, kids play without refs and by their own rules. They round up their friends. And they play in a quiet street, a playground, or a nearby park.

Pro teams run or throw the ball into the **end zone**. Or they kick **field goals** to score. But you can play any way you want in your neighborhood.

Huddle up. Let's play!

FUN FACT

No one really invented football. It developed from a blend of different field games.

TEAM DRAFT

In street football, you need a **quarterback** to throw, and people to catch the ball and run.

Round up all the kids you can find—even ones you don't know well. Street football is a good way to make new friends.

FUN FACT

In street football, you don't tackle. You usually play two-hand touch. You can also hang rags or flags from your pocket or belt. If someone pulls your flag, the play is over.

In street football, you could play in teams of two. Switch off playing quarterback and **running back** or **receiver**.

If you have five kids, you could have one quarterback for both teams.

FUN FACT

Pro football teams score six points if they make a touchdown. And they can go for extra points. In street football, you decide how much you want touchdowns to be worth.

GOAL LINES

A lamppost could become the **goal line**. And each team could have four chances to get the ball there and score.

Now, let's get this **offense** rolling!

FUN FACT

You can use chalk to make a goal line on the ground.

Running backs must outrun defenders to score. Practice by holding the ball and racing a friend to the goal line.

THE HANDOFF

Make a pocket for the ball if you're the runner. Bend your elbows. Hold one arm out in front with your palm down. The other arm is below, palm up.

Tuck the ball close to your chest. Then run!

THE PASS

To throw, bend your knees a bit. Make a V with your thumb and pointer finger near the tip of the ball. Cover the laces with your other fingers.

Hold your elbow up and back over your shoulder. Step toward your receiver. Then, let the ball spin off your fingers.

FUN FACT

If you throw with your right arm, take a step forward with your left foot. When throwing with your left hand, step with your right foot.

FUN FACT

More and more girls are playing football in high schools across the country.

THE CATCH

To catch above your waist, place the tips of your thumbs and pointer fingers together. Form a diamond. Catch the tip of the football through that hole.

To catch a low ball, keep your thumbs up. Hold your pinkies together.

SUPER BOWL FUN DAY!

Touchdown! Every day can be like Super Bowl Sunday. Cheer for your friends when they make an awesome play. Play safe, and have a blast!

FUN FACT

The National Football League (NFL) is rooting for you to exercise 60 minutes a day. Running, throwing and catching a football gets you up and moving. Exercise is good for you!

21

GLOSSARY

end zone (END zohn): The place at both ends of the football field where points are scored.

field goal (FEELD GOHL): A field goal is when a team kicks the ball through the goal posts. If the ball sails over the crossbar, the team scores three points.

goal line (GOHL LINE): The goal line is the line between the playing field and the end zone.

huddle (HUD-uhl): When the offense gathers together to talk and prepare for the next play.

offense (AWF-ents): The team with the ball that is trying to score.

pro (PROH): A *pro* is short for a "professional." It is an athlete who is paid to play the sport.

quarterback (KWOR-tur-bak): The quarterback starts each play on offense. After grabbing the ball from the center, the quarterback can hand the ball to another player, throw it, or keep it and run.

receiver (re-SEE-vur): A player who catches passes from the quarterback and tries to score touchdowns. Receivers are some of the fastest players on the team.

running back (RUN-ing BAK): A player who takes the ball from the quarterback and runs it down field. Running backs can also block or catch passes.

tackle (TAK-uhl): To knock or throw a ball carrier to the ground.

touchdown (TUCH-down): A team scores six points when it moves the ball into the other team's end zone. A player carries the ball over the goal line or catches a pass in the end zone.

TO LEARN MORE

In the Library

Jacobs, Greg. *The Everything Kids' Football Book: All-time Greats, Legendary Teams, and Today's Favorite Players–with Tips on Playing Like a Pro*. Avon, MA: Adams Media, 2016.

Sports Illustrated Kids. *1st and 10: Top 10 Lists of Everything in Football*. New York, NY: Liberty Street, 2016.

Thomas, Keltie. *How Football Works*. Toronto, Ontario: Maple Tree Press, 2010.

On the Web

Visit our Web page for lots of links about street football:

childsworld.com/links

Note to parents, teachers, and librarians: We routinely verify our Web links to make sure they are safe, active sites—so encourage your readers to check them out!

INDEX